INVESTIGATION OF ROAD TRAFFIC FATALITIES

AN ATLAS

FORENSIC PATHOLOGY ATLASES
CAUSES OF DEATH SERIES

Series Editor: Jay Dix

Asphyxia and Drowning: An Atlas
Jay Dix, Michael Graham and Randy Hanzlick

Investigation of Road Traffic Fatalities: An Atlas
Jay Dix, Michael Graham and Randy Hanzlick

Time of Death, Decomposition and Identification: An Atlas
Jay Dix and Michael Graham

INVESTIGATION OF ROAD TRAFFIC FATALITIES

AN ATLAS

JAY DIX,
MICHAEL GRAHAM
AND
RANDY HANZLICK

CRC Press

Boca Raton   London   New York   Washington, D.C.

Library of Congress Cataloging-in-Publication Data

Catalog record is available from the Library of Congress.

The CD-ROM version of this book, showing the photographs in full color without text, is available by writing to Academic Information Systems, 3205 Woodvalley Way, Columbia, MO 65203, or by calling (573) 882-1209.

No claim to original U.S. Government works
International Standard Book Number 0-8493-2368-1
Printed in the United States of America 1 2 3 4 5 6 7 8 9 0
Printed on acid-free paper

Preface

This atlas is written for medical examiners/coroners (ME/Cs), medicolegal death investigators (DIs), and law enforcement personnel who work with medical examiners and coroners during the investigation of road traffic fatalities (RTFs). A RTF occurs when death is due to injuries caused by one or more moving vehicle(s) designed for use on roadways. For the most part, these vehicles are cars, vans, motorcycles and trucks of various sizes. This atlas does not address other types of vehicle-related fatalities such as those involving trains, aircraft, boats, all-terrain vehicles, or injuries caused by non-moving vehicles (such as crush injury from a car falling off a jack). The information provided in this atlas concentrates on the types of issues that face medical examiners and coroners in determining the nature and extent of injuries and the cause, manner and circumstances of death — not on the duties of the police or law enforcement agency that is responsible for documenting the basic facts of the incident (and perhaps reconstructing the events).

R.H.

The Authors

Jay Dix, M.D. is Medical Examiner for Boone County, Missouri, and Associate Professor of Pathology/Chief of Forensic Pathology at the University of Missouri School of Medicine in Columbia. Dr. Dix has authored several outstanding books in the field of pathology and serves as a consultant to attorneys in both civil and criminal matters, and to coroners throughout mid-Missouri.

Michael Graham, M.D. is the Chief Medical Examiner for the City of St. Louis, Missouri; Professor of Pathology at St. Louis University Health Sciences Center; and Co-Director of its Division of Forensic Pathology. He also serves as the Secretary-Treasurer of the National Association of Medical Examiners, a member of the Forensic Committee of the College of American Pathologists and is a former officer of the Pathology/Biology Section of the American Academy of Forensic Sciences. Writer and editor of numerous scientific papers, book chapters and books, Dr. Graham is also on the Editorial Board of the *American Journal of Forensic Medicine and Pathology*. He is certified in anatomic, clinical and forensic pathology by the American Board of Pathology.

Randy Hanzlick, M.D. is Chief Medical Examiner for Fulton County, Georgia; Associate Professor of Forensic Pathology, Emory University School of Medicine, Atlanta; and Forensic Pathologist, Centers for Disease Control and Prevention, Atlanta. He has authored more than 150 scientific medical publications including articles, letters, chapters, books and manuals. His major areas of interest include forensic pathology and death investigation systems, training and guidelines. A board-certified forensic pathologist, Dr. Hanzlick is active in the National Association of Medical Examiners, the American Academy of Forensic Sciences and the College of American Pathologists.

Table of Contents

Road Traffic Fatalities

Cause, Manner and Circumstances of Death

Since the medical examiner/coroner's (ME/C's) main duty is to determine the cause, manner and circumstances of death, specific definition of these terms may be helpful.

The cause of death is the condition or sequence of conditions, e.g., injuries in road traffic fatalities (RTFs), that adversely acts on the human body to result in death. The cause of death usually differs from the cause of the traffic incident, which often involves some human behavioral factor (such as drinking and driving), vehicular problem (such as faulty braking system) or roadway or environmental condition (such as wet roadway during a rainstorm). A simple example of a typical cause of death that could apply to a driver who died when the car struck a tree is:

> Intrathoracic hemorrhage
> > Due to: Ruptured aorta
> > Due to: Blunt force injury of the thorax
> > Due to: Motor vehicle crash (This may be added here or in another section of the death certificate that describes how the injuries occurred.)

In essence, for RTFs, the cause of death is a medical description of the injury event, bodily trauma and related fatal derangements that caused the death.

The manner of death is a classification of death based on whether death was brought about by an injury and whether the injury was intentional or unintentional. The options for manner of death are natural, accidental,

1

homicide, suicide and undetermined. In an apparent RTF, any of these manners of death may be applicable, although most are classified as accidents because most are unintentional. A manner of death of "accident" does not necessarily indicate that there has not been some violation of the criminal code.

The manner of death is classified as natural if death resulted solely from disease or age-related processes. In some apparent RTFs there may actually be no significant injuries and the apparent "accident" may have been brought about by a fatal natural disease in the driver (such as a heart attack). For example, a car being driven by an elderly person may be seen to gradually move forward from a stop light and run into a tree with no indication that the driver tried to avoid the crash. It may turn out that there are no significant bodily injuries and that a myocardial infarction (heart attack) is discovered at autopsy. In such a case, the manner of death would be classified as natural. Cases such as this provide one reason why autopsies are commonly performed on drivers who die in apparent RTFs. In other cases, the vehicular crash may be caused by a natural disease (heart attack leading to unconsciousness), although death is caused by injuries sustained in the crash.

If investigation determines that death did result from injuries sustained in the road traffic incident and there is no indication that the crash was caused on purpose (intentionally), the manner of death is classified as accident. In essence, death was unintentional or unpredictable and caused by injury that occurred during the incident.

Some RTFs involve a specific intent of the driver to kill him/herself, such as by running into a concrete bridge abutment at high speed. Although such cases are uncommon, the manner of death would be classified as suicide if sufficient facts could be developed during the investigation to show that the victim intended to kill him/herself or do self-harm.

If the death of one person is intentionally caused by another person, or the death of one person results from a volitional (voluntary) act of another person, the manner of death is usually classified as homicide by the ME/C. As far as RTFs are concerned, in most jurisdictions the manner of death is classified as homicide only if investigation shows that the at-fault party was intentionally trying to kill or harm the victim (such as intentionally running over someone after an argument). However, most states have laws that specifically define "vehicular homicide," and the definition may apply even though there was no specific intent to kill anyone. For example, a pedestrian death caused by a drunk driver or an at-fault driver who flees the scene of an accident may qualify for the legal definition of vehicular homicide. Whether or not the ME/C classifies the death as homicide in such cases depends on the extent of known facts, jurisdictional procedures and the philosophy of the ME/C. Most ME/Cs, however, prefer to classify "vehicular homicides" as accidents and let the district attorney and court decide if the term "vehicular homicide" is applicable for court purposes and possible prosecution.

In some cases, the manner of death cannot be determined. Injuries may be minor and disease extensive. Or, there may be some indication of suicide that cannot be proven with the preponderance of evidence. Other possibilities exist as well, and in such cases the manner of death may be classified as undetermined.

Thus, an apparent RTF may ultimately be classified as any of the five manners of death: accident, homicide, suicide, natural or undetermined. The need to determine manner of death is another reason why RTFs are investigated and why autopsies are commonly performed, especially on drivers and pedestrians.

For statistical purposes, tabulations of "fatal traffic accidents" are usually based only on those RTFs that have been classified as accidents. Of course, if the manner of death has been classified as natural it means that the apparent traffic incident did not actually cause death. Rather, death was due to natural causes but the initial circumstances appeared as a road traffic incident and possible RTF. Such a case would not be classified as an RTF because the road traffic incident did not cause death.

Clarification of the circumstances of death from the ME/C perspective is directed mainly at determining how and where the fatal injuries occurred. For example, the death certificate requires that a statement be given to explain "how injury occurred," the "place of injury," and the "address where injury occurred." It is the ME/C's responsibility to obtain complete and accurate information about these data items. For example, the phrase "driver of car in car-to-car head-on collision" might be used to explain how injury occurred, the place of injury might be listed as "2 Lane County Road," and the address where injury occurred might be indicated as "Mile Marker 26, Old Alabama Road."

The other major aspect of clarifying the circumstances of death from the ME/C standpoint (other than determining the cause and manner of death) is to determine what decedent factors may have played a role in the accident, such as determining whether a driver or pedestrian was intoxicated at the time of the incident. In general, the ultimate determination of whether vehicle factors or road and environment problems contributed to the incident is the responsibility of the investigating law enforcement agency or traffic accident reconstruction specialist, not the ME/C.

RTF Investigation vs. RTF Reconstruction

There is a difference between road traffic accident investigation and reconstruction. In brief, from the ME/C standpoint, investigation consists mainly of documenting the basic facts of the incident in order to determine the nature of injuries and the cause, manner and circumstances of death, and to collect evidence in appropriate cases where criminal acts may have been involved (such as hit-and-run cases where the at-fault driver flees the scene). Reconstruction is a more extensive endeavor that requires retrospective analysis of the facts and the application of traffic engineering science to more fully clarify the crash dynamics, vehicular/bodily movements and sequence of events. The basic duties of the ME/C relate to investigation, not necessarily reconstruction. However, a general discussion of reconstruction may be helpful.

In his book, *Motor Vehicle Accident Reconstruction and Cause Analysis*, Rudolf Limpert describes five specific objectives of traffic accident reconstruction:

- Collision analysis
- Injury analysis
- Accident avoidance analysis
- Injury avoidance analysis
- Accident causation ranking

Collision analysis includes documentation of the basic aspects of the incident such as vehicle directions, speeds, impact points, crush damage, rotations and final resting points. For the most part, this is what the investigating law enforcement officer documents during the routine investigation of road traffic incidents.

Injury analysis is directed at description of how injuries were produced, assessment of occupant motion and contact with the vehicle and other objects, the role of safety devices and analysis of specific information on the nature of bodily injuries. It is this last component that is mainly provided by the ME/C through death investigation and autopsy.

Accident avoidance analysis is concerned mainly with analysis of factors to determine if and how the accident may have been avoided or reduced in severity.

Injury avoidance analysis involves investigation of all possible factors that may be addressed to prevent bodily injury such as analysis of safety devices, interior vehicle design and similar features.

Accident causation ranking is a method for ranking the relative importance of factors related to the driver, vehicle, roadway and environment in having caused the incident.

Most routine traffic accident investigations include only basic collision analysis (usually performed by law enforcement) and injury analysis to the extent of identifying and documenting the nature of bodily injuries (usually determined by the medical examiner, forensic pathologist or coroner's pathologist). The other components of injury analysis, accident avoidance analysis, and accident causation ranking are not routinely used and usually come into play when the incident results in legal proceedings and subsequent investigations by the parties in the case, or for automotive safety and design studies and research.

Limpert also describes the basic elements of an accident reconstruction as:

- The facts section
- The engineering analysis section
- The witness statement section

The *facts section* generally includes information derived from observations and measurements related to any vehicles, the roadway and victims. Such information is routinely obtained by the investigating law enforcement agency in virtually all traffic accidents.

The *engineering analysis section* includes use of mathematical equations, tests and data interpretation. Engineering analysis may not be routinely used and is called into play in selected cases, although it is common for law enforcement agencies to use some standard mathematical formulas for estimating vehicle speed and other parameters.

The *witness statement section* includes accounts of people who report what they saw and heard (or what they think they saw and heard!). This is an integral part of all traffic accident investigations but it must be remembered that witness accounts are often erroneous, especially in regard to estimated speeds. Witness accounts must be weighed against information developed in other elements of the investigation.

Limpert points out that there is no formal course of study in traffic accident reconstruction, and the basis for serving as an expert in this field is a combination of adequate background education and experience in doing the job. He states that a bachelor's degree in physical/mechanical, automotive or civil engineering along with 2 years of accident reconstruction experience are viewed as minimal requirements to serve as an expert witness in court. Many DIs, medical examiners and coroners may not specifically meet these requirements. Thus, the challenges and duties of traffic accident reconstruction frequently fall to parties other than the ME/C or DI.

Finally, Limpert categorizes the basic components of road traffic incidents as:

- Driver
- Vehicle(s)
- Roadway
- Environment (which may include human objects, such as pedestrians)

In this book, we will concentrate on the various aspects of each of these components that are particularly relevant to the ME/C or DI when conducting investigations of RTFs. For an extensive discussion of traffic accident reconstruction, the reader is referred to Limpert's book.

Jurisdictional and Statutory Considerations

In most states, the death investigation laws place injury-related deaths under the jurisdiction of the medical examiner or coroner for the purposes of investigation of the cause and manner of death and clarification of the circumstances surrounding death. Duties also usually include completion of investigative reports, reports of postmortem examination (if any) and the death certificate.

Because RTFs involve injury, they usually are investigated by the medical examiner or coroner. However, not all states are the same. For example, in Utah, the medical examiner does not have authority to investigate RTFs. In other states, the medical examiner or coroner may have to certify such deaths, but law may restrict the performance of an autopsy to selected types of circumstances. The important point to know is that familiarity with local and state death investigation laws and practices is extremely important so that any death investigation is performed in compliance with the law and to the extent needed based on specific case circumstances. Be sure to read the death investigation laws that apply to the jurisdiction where you work. Most coroners and medical examiners have copies of these laws. The laws also are usually available from the Secretary of State and many states now have all of their current statutes available on the Internet.

It is also important to know whether jurisdiction of the death investigation belongs to the county where the RTF occurred or the county where death occurred; they may differ. Be sure to know the details of your own state's death investigation laws. There also may be some areas such as federal property, Indian reservations or other areas within the boundaries of your jurisdiction that you do not have legal authority to investigate. Finally, the law enforcement agency responsible for investigating RTFs may also vary depending on state law and the type of road (interstate highway, city street, etc.) or location of the roadway. Be sure to be familiar with all of these details as they apply to the city, county, region or state where you will be investigating RTFs.

Who Usually Does What?

In general, the law enforcement agency is responsible for documenting, diagramming and determining the basic circumstances and sequence of events related to an RTF. Emphasis is on documenting the basic facts of the incident, who was involved, who witnessed the event, who may have been at fault, who was injured or killed, and who may or may not need to be taken into custody for some violation of the law. Most law enforcement agencies use a standard reporting form, based on a model uniform traffic accident report form, which contains standardized questions about the vehicles, roadways, people involved, the weather and a space for drawing a diagram of the incident. In many jurisdictions, law enforcement officers who investigate RTFs have had special training in traffic accident reconstruction and, in some areas, police departments have specialists who do nothing but conduct investigations of RTFs. Of course, law enforcement officers perform these duties in almost all motor vehicle accidents whether or not there is a fatality.

The ME/C or DI is called in when a death occurs and is concerned mainly with confirming that death has occurred, establishing the identity of the deceased, examining the body, documenting its appearance, determining the nature of wounds and disease that may be present to explain why death occurred (and perhaps why the RTF incident occurred) and to determine the specific cause, manner and circumstances of death for the purposes of completion of the death certificate. The ME/C or DI may also be responsible for notifying the next of kin of the death, but in many areas this procedure is done by the law enforcement agency. It should be determined at the scene who will do the notification, and the notification should be documented in the case record.

Proper coordination is needed between the ME/C (or the DI) and the law enforcement officer investigating the incident. It is very important for all involved parties to discuss in advance exactly who will perform which tasks and take responsibility for them. In most cases, law enforcement is responsible for controlling and investigating the general scene area and the ME/C is responsible for the body and its immediate surroundings.

Basic Caveats

It is not our intent to provide extensive discussion of crash dynamics and traffic accident reconstruction. However, there are a few basic principles that generally hold true:

1. In general, when a large, heavy vehicle is in a collision with a smaller, lighter vehicle, people in the smaller (lighter) vehicle will be at greater risk for serious injury. (Basically, the bigger vehicle often wins.)
2. In general, people who remain in a vehicle are at less risk for serious injury than those who are ejected from a vehicle. This is one reason why front windshield glass is laminated so it cracks and deforms, but does not usually shatter at relatively low speeds (less than 30 mph).
3. There are characteristic, somewhat predictable injuries that occur in various types of RTF situations. (These are discussed below.)
4. Motorcyclists are at much greater risk (at least three times greater risk) for fatal injury than drivers of cars because they have little protection and they are usually ejected from the motorcycle, which also increases risk of serious injury.
5. The potential for serious injury is often expressed in terms of the change in velocity — usually referred to as "delta-V." For example, if a person were driving at 60 mph and came to an abrupt stop when the car hits a cement wall, delta-V would be approximately 60 mph. Using equations, delta-V can be mathematically converted to other units of force such as g-force (multiples of the force of gravity) or pounds per square inch (psi). Human tolerance levels to injury forces expressed in such terms (g-force or psi) have been well established. Thus, the nature of injuries as determined by the ME/C may be used by the reconstructionist or engineer to estimate forces, calculate vehicle speeds or reconstruct various sequences in the incident — any or all of which may become major issues in legal proceedings. This emphasizes how important it is that the ME/C or pathologist accurately describe and document the nature and extent of injuries on the body.
6. There are many terms that have very specific meanings and connotations in traffic accident analysis. Awareness of this is important so that specific words are not misused or misinterpreted. For example, tire marks on the roadway may be used to reconstruct vehicle movement, speed, direction of travel, braking and other events. There are several subtypes of tire marks, each of which has a specific connotation and name, such as print marks, tire rubber prints, tread prints, imprints, flat-tire marks, post-crash flat tire marks, yaw marks, grinding marks,

spin marks, skid marks, shadow marks, acceleration spin marks, wheels-locked grindings marks and heating tire marks. Discussion of these types is beyond the scope of this book, but it behooves the ME/C or DI to know that reconstruction terminology is complex and proper knowledge is needed to use it appropriately — not just for tire marks, but also for many other aspects of the investigation.

7. Drivers who cause fatal accidents and adult pedestrians who are struck by vehicles are often intoxicated or otherwise impaired and/or acting in a reckless fashion.

Motor vehicle "accident" reconstruction is a specialized area of expertise that requires knowledge of engineering and physics. There are many self-proclaimed experts in traffic accident reconstruction and the ME/C or DI definitely runs the risk of being asked questions that fall outside of his/her scope of expertise. An immense body of knowledge exists about the biomechanics of bodily injury and vehicle damage that occur in vehicular accidents. This atlas attempts only to address the very basic issues that the ME/C or DI commonly addresses. ME/Cs and DIs are advised to be conservative in their approaches to investigations and to be sure to refer questions and issues to an appropriate expert with special knowledge, experience, and training for the issue at hand.

General Classifications of RTFs

It is useful to classify deaths involving RTFs into the following, based on the status of the deceased:

1. Driver (operator)
2. Occupant (passenger)
3. Pedestrian (on-foot, lying in roadway, etc.)

It is also helpful to classify the circumstances of the fatal event as:

1. Vehicle striking fixed object (may involve ejection)
2. Vehicle losing control with rollover (may involve ejection)
3. Collision of two or more vehicles; head-on, rear-end, side-impact ("T-bone"), tangential, sideswipe (may involve ejection)
4. Vehicle impact with pedestrian
5. Vehicle enters an unusual and hazardous environment (submerged in water, etc.)

Common Questions to be Answered During RTF Investigations

During the investigation of a RTF, the following questions are commonly encountered. Italicized questions are those that the ME/C and/or DI plays a major role in addressing or answering:

Concerning the victim:

1. *Was there some problem, disease or other factor involving the victim that may have caused or contributed to the incident (such as intoxication, heart attack before the crash, etc.)?*
2. *Was there any evidence that the incident was intentionally caused by the victim (i.e., attempt to commit suicide)?*
3. *Is there any evidence that the traffic incident was the terminal outcome of some other incident (such as the driver having been shot earlier)?*
4. Was there any evidence that the victim was aware of the impending incident and tried to avoid it (i.e., tire marks from applying brakes)?
5. *Did injuries cause death, or did death occur before the crash?*
6. *How long did it take for the victim to die?*
7. *How long would the victim have been conscious and aware of pain after the crash?*
8. *If the vehicle caught fire, did the fire play a role in causing death?*
9. Which objects came into contact with the victim?
10. *Which impacts caused or contributed to death?*
11. *Were there any injuries that appeared to be caused by safety devices such as seat belts or air bags?*
12. *If a pedestrian in a hit-and-run incident, is there any evidence that may be helpful in identifying a suspect vehicle (and driver)?*

Concerning the vehicle:

1. Did any vehicular malfunctions or defects (steering system, braking system, tire problems) cause or contribute to the fatal event?
2. Was there any evidence of malfunction of safety devices, such as seat belts and airbags?
3. Is there any indication of a flaw in vehicular design or construction?
4. If the vehicle caught fire, did the fire start spontaneously from the vehicle itself or from another source (such as arson)?

Concerning the environment:

1. Did any road conditions cause or contribute to the incident?
2. Did weather conditions cause or contribute to the incident?
3. Did any other factors such as lighting, signage or traffic control devices cause or contribute to the incident?

It can be seen that some of these questions require information about the body (autopsy) in order to be addressed; they are the primary responsibility of the ME/C. Others require careful scene investigation and evaluation of the vehicle or other evidence that does not necessarily involve the examination of the body and may fall into the domain of the law enforcement agency. In general, the DI is concerned mostly with those questions that have directly to do with the body and mechanisms of injury, while the law enforcement agency is usually concerned more with the factors involving the roadway, vehicle characteristics and environmental conditions. All factors are of interest to, and must be considered by the ME/C or DI, but the extent of concern and follow-up concerning the nonhuman factors necessarily fall mainly to the investigating law enforcement agency.

Injuries Caused by Safety/Restraint Devices

Injuries caused by seat belts typically include:

*   Abrasions and/or bruises on the skin surfaces in positions which correspond to where the belt comes into contact with the body
*   Fracture of the collar bone and/or ribs
*   Lacerations of liver or other abdominal injuries from "submarining" under the belt
*   Occasional pelvic or spinal column fractures

Injuries caused by air bags are usually minor but may include:

*   Ejection from the vehicle (if seat belt not worn)
*   Blunt force injuries to small children, which may be severe or lethal
*   Facial, cervical or thoracic bruises, lacerations or fractures
*   Rarely: severe eye injury, airway trauma or lung collapse

Many airbags have a coating of talc or starch to facilitate opening of the airbag. This material may be found on the skin of accident victims.

Basic Injury Mechanisms

RTFs generally involve one or more of the following types of injury.

1. *Direct impact.* This results from direct impact between vehicle components and the body or the body and other objects. Typical examples include a pedestrian being struck by a vehicle; a pedestrian body impacting with other objects such as the roadway; or an occupant sustaining a direct impact by intrusion of the door from an impact to the side of the car, caused by another vehicle.

2. *Deceleration injury.* This occurs when the body is moving and then comes to a sudden stop — usually when it impacts with some other object. The body is "thrown forward" or continues in the direction of vehicle movement, and impacts with vehicle components as a result of the impact.

3. *Positional injuries.* The relative position of a vehicle and a human body may cause death by virtue of the position in which the body ultimately comes to rest. For example, a car may come to rest on a body, or a body may be suspended or compressed in a vehicle in such a position that the victim may not be able to breathe adequately. There may be no significant disruption of tissues due to injury, but death may still occur.

4. *Exacerbation of underlying disease.* Minor trauma may precipitate a heart attack or other "natural" event. For example, we have seen a case in which a passenger received minor injury in a "fender bender," opened the door and exited the car by himself, walked around for a few minutes, then collapsed to the ground after suffering a typical hypertensive hemorrhage in his brain, apparently brought about by the stress of the seemingly "minor" incident.

5. *Unusual environments.* In some circumstances, the body (with or without the vehicle) may end up in a hostile and unsafe environment. For example, a person who was ejected from a vehicle into a lake may actually die from drowning or hypothermia.

For pedestrians, other classifications of injury type are also helpful.

1. *Primary impact.* These wounds are caused by direct initial impact of the vehicle with the pedestrian.

2. *Secondary impacts.* These occur after the primary impact, usually when the body is thrown onto the vehicle and impacts with the hood, windshield or roof.

3. *Tertiary impacts.* These occur after secondary impacts and may result from landing on the roadway or ground, or being struck by subsequent vehicles.

It is important to realize that the direction in which a pedestrian's body will travel after primary impact depends on where the pedestrian is struck. If struck below the center of gravity (approximately waist level) while standing or walking, the pedestrian will tend to be "under-run" by the vehicle and have secondary impacts with the vehicle (such as the hood, windshield, or top of the vehicle). If struck above the center of gravity (above the waist) the body may be thrown forward in the direction that the vehicle was traveling and is commonly run over. Vehicles with high front ends (such as large trucks) tend to throw the victim forward, because they strike the victim above the center of gravity, while those with lower front ends (such as standard cars) tend to cause the pedestrian to fly up onto the hood or windshield, because they typically strike the victim below the center of gravity. Children are typically struck above their centers of gravity and thrown forward and downward.

Most fatal injuries resulting from RTFs are due to blunt force impacts that cause tissue disruption (bruises, lacerations, fractures, abrasions). Some fatalities, however, may be due to other mechanisms such as asphyxia, sharp force wounds (cuts/stabs), other penetrating injuries, burns, smoke inhalation or rarer conditions. Specific injury types are described below.

Common but Critical Investigative Mistakes

Several things can happen (or not happen!) during an RTF investigation that can severely hamper the investigation or cause erroneous conclusions. They include:

- *Failure to collect the clothing.* It is important to safeguard and collect the clothing, particularly when a pedestrian road traffic victim has been taken to the hospital. The clothing may have markings (grease, torn defects, paint, etc.) that enable reconstruction of impact sites, clarification of the nature and pattern of injuries or comparison to clothing fragments found on a suspect vehicle. Shoes may bear markings that indicate whether the foot (shoe) was on the gas or brake pedal.
- *Failure to examine the helmet in motorcycle crashes.* The helmet may bear signs of impact when the head does not. This can be helpful in reconstructing how injuries may have occurred.

- *Failure to review medical records and ambulance trip sheets.* Especially when death occurs in the hospital (which may be many days or weeks after injury), examination of the medical records and ambulance trip sheet may be the only way to assess the original injuries and their outcomes and sequelae. In other cases, review of the medical record may be important to assess the possibility that some problem with medical treatment played a role in the death, or to distinguish between traffic-related injury and injuries caused by medical treatment (such as incisions, airway trauma from intubation, etc.).
- *Failure to review the police accident report.* The report may contain information that is very helpful in interpreting injuries. It is also helpful to verify whether the "final" report contains facts that are consistent with those initially obtained at the time of the incident.
- *Failure to obtain hospital specimens if death occurred at the hospital.* Blood and other specimens obtained at the time of admission to the hospital may be the only suitable specimens for performing toxicology or blood typing tests (to compare with blood at the scene or on a suspect vehicle). They should routinely be obtained if death occurs in the hospital after a traffic incident.
- *Failure to obtain an adequate background medical/social/psychiatric history.* Especially in circumstances where there is no apparent reason for the accident, in pedestrian deaths or when the victim was the sole occupant of a vehicle and was apparently at fault, it is very important to determine whether the traffic incident represented an act of suicide. This may involve delving into the victim's psychosocial history and obtaining appropriate medical records or other information from professionals who had treated or evaluated the victim.
- *Failure to investigate related scene locations.* In some cases, especially those in which suicide is a possibility, it may be necessary not only to inspect the vehicle thoroughly for suicide notes, but also to inspect the home, workplace, or other places recently visited by the victim.

Factors that Raise Suspicion of Suicide

Some circumstances should raise suspicion that the RTF was a suicidal act:

- Dead-center impact in the front of the vehicle
- No seat belt or safety devices used
- High speed
- No apparent reason for the crash
- No evidence of attempts to avoid or brake

- Collision into a heavy, fixed object
- Nobody else in the vehicle
- History of suicide attempts or gestures
- Swerve into oncoming traffic for no apparent reason
- Pedestrian fatalities in which victim is struck head-on, or was lying on the roadway when struck, or appeared to have "jumped" or "darted" into traffic

Suicide by motor vehicle may be very difficult to prove. Very thorough investigation is required. Most states have laws, case law or legal opinion that the weight of evidence required to classify the manner of death as suicide cannot just be "more likely than not," but rather that the "preponderance of evidence" (reasonable certainty) is the required burden of proof to classify a death as suicide.

Typical RTF Injuries

Several types of injuries are classic and almost pathognomonic for, or extremely typical of, specific injury mechanisms:

- *Glass dicing.* These consist of angulated cuts on the skin caused by tempered glass chips from shattered side or rear windows. They may occur in vehicle occupants or pedestrians. The tempered glass in side and rear windows is made to shatter into tiny pieces when it breaks, and glass dicing is caused by this type of glass. It typically is seen on the head or face.
- *"Brush burn" sliding abrasion (road rash).* This usually consists of large, map-like or streak-like areas of abrasion (scraping off of the skin's top layer) caused by impact and gliding along the road surface. Depending on the nature of the road surface, it may have a very distinctive appearance that reflects the character of the road surface, and may contain adherent or imbedded particulate matter from the road surface.
- *Pebbling abrasions.* These consist of multiple small, round-to-rectangular abrasions on the skin that typically occur in clusters and result from impact on a rough road surface, such as asphalt (black top) or surfaces with high gravel, stone or coarse aggregate content.
- *Glass scratches and superficial cuts.* These usually consist of multiple, parallel, usually vertical superficial cuts or scratches in the skin, often accompanied by some abrasion. Glass scratches usually result when the forehead or other body part impacts with the cracked glass in the laminated front windshield and is caused by a gliding of the tissue

over the fractured glass. The front windshield consists of multiple glass and plastic layers and is designed to crack, not shatter, and remain in place at impact speeds of up to approximately 30 mph. This helps the occupant to be retained in the vehicle rather than ejected (because ejection increases the risk of fatal injury). It also prevents serious neck and head cuts as a result of the head protruding through the glass.

- *Annular avulsions or decollement.* This injury usually occurs when a tire rotates on the skin, especially on an upper or lower extremity (arm or leg). The rotational force of the tire causes the upper layer of skin to be pulled away from deeper layers, creating a pocket-like space in the tissues. In severe cases, all of the soft tissue may be pulled away (avulsed) from the underlying bone.

- *Stretch injury.* Especially in pedestrians or other victims who are run over by vehicles, there may be injuries that represent extreme stretching of tissues. It is not uncommon for the skin of the groin to be split open in pedestrians who are struck from the rear, and the abdominal organs frequently bulge through the wound. "Acute stretch marks," similar in appearance to those sometimes seen on the skin of obese people, but more yellow/red/orange in appearance, may occur in any area of skin that undergoes severe stretching, as on the abdomen or flank in pedestrians who are struck from the rear or when the skin is extensively stretched by being run over by a tire/vehicle.

- *Tread marks.* Impact by a tire, or being run over by a tire may result in abrasions or bruises on the skin that leave a distinctive pattern from the tire in question. Usually this occurs when people are run over, but it may result from tire impact to an upright victim.

- *Traumatic fat necrosis pockets.* Direct and extensive impact to soft tissues may so traumatize the fat beneath the skin as to liquify it. This may create palpable pockets beneath the skin, which contain liquified fat that has the appearance of chicken broth. These pockets may also contain significant hemorrhage or cause death by allowing fat to enter the circulation and result in a fatal fat embolism (fat in the bloodstream).

- *Telescoped fractures.* Particularly on the upper and lower extremities (arms, forearms, thighs, legs) there may be fractures of the long bones in which the fractured ends of the bones glide past each other causing the arm or leg to become much shorter. These typically occur when the thighs impact with the dashboard or the arms or forearms sustain impacts end-on (along the direction of the bone).

- *Steering wheel injury.* The steering wheel or center post of the steering wheel may leave distinctive patterned contusions on the skin or cause significant internal injury. However, distinctive wounds on the skin surface are much less common than they were in the past because steering columns are no longer rigid and now made to collapse on impact.

- *Atlanto-occipital dislocation.* The forces in many traffic accidents are extensive enough that impacts to the face or head sometimes cause complete fracture/separation of the junction of the upper cervical spine and base of the skull, which can cause fatal brainstem/spinal cord injury. Lower cervical spine fractures are also common and usually result from hyperextension of the neck when the face/head sustains an impact. These injuries are relatively common in fatally struck pedestrians.

- *Deceleration injury.* The typical deceleration injury in a RTF victim occurs in a driver or occupant of a vehicle that has sustained a front-end collision and comes to an abrupt stop. The typical and classic finding is a chest full of blood caused by rupture of the aorta near the junction of the left subclavian artery. This is often associated with extensive rib fractures and fracture of the sternum. Typically, there are transverse fractures of the sternum and bilateral, multiple rib fractures that tend to occur along the anterolateral aspect of the ribs, but may also occur elsewhere.

- *Bumper injuries.* On pedestrians, these may include patterned contusions with a distinctive pattern on the skin, but more often consist of fractures caused by direct bumper impact. They usually occur on the leg below the knee and often are compounded with splitting of the overlying skin. The height of the fracture above the bottom of the foot may allow some estimation of whether the driver tried to brake. During extreme braking, the bumper may dip and cause fractures closer to the ground than would occur if the driver was not braking. Thus, measuring the exact location of these fractures is helpful. Sometimes, however, similar fractures may occur if the foot is planted and the body rotates, but there is not a direct impact at the fracture site. Thus, fractures of the leg do not prove impact with a bumper. If bumper fractures are present on only one leg or are present at different heights on each leg, it may be that the pedestrian was walking or running when struck. It has been stated that bumper fractures do not usually occur unless the vehicle was traveling at about 15 mph or faster.

- *Hip fracture.* In pedestrians or occupants whose leg or thigh is thrust into the dashboard or other front wall component, the head of the femur may be pushed out of its socket or the femoral neck may fracture. This often causes the entire thigh and leg to have a shorter appearance than normal and to be rotated away from the body. Another injury produced by impact of the knee with the dashboard is splitting of the distal femur by the patella (kneecap) being driven in between the forked ends (condyles) of the femur.

- *Embedded materials.* It is not uncommon for foreign materials such as paint, plastic parts from vehicles or loose items on the roadway to be pressed into or embedded in the skin or wounds. All efforts should be made to ensure that these items are not lost during movement of the body, as they may be critical in reconstructing the accident or identifying a responsible vehicle.

- *Cardiac injuries.* When there is a major blunt impact to the front of the chest (anterior thorax), it is not uncommon for the anterior wall of the right ventricle of the heart to tear, allowing blood to fill the heart sac (pericardium). The wall (septum) between the right and left atrium sometimes also tears with similar types of impacts. Occasionally, severe compressive impacts to the abdomen may be associated with tears of the inner surface within the right atrium of the heart, caused by transmitted hydrostatic forces overdistending the chamber of the heart.

- *Other visceral injuries.* Major blunt impacts also frequently result in lacerations to the liver and/or spleen, and it is not uncommon for the attachment points of the lungs (the pulmonary hilum) to be torn with damage to the underlying blood vessels.

- *Pelvic fractures.* The pelvis is essentially a ring-like bone that may fracture when impacted, essentially breaking the "ring." Usually, there has been a direct impact to the pelvis, but not always. Quite often, the fracture sites are displaced and may tear adjacent blood vessels or the urinary bladder.

- *Head injuries.* In most fatal road traffic incidents there is often some degree of head injury. This may consist of scalp hemorrhage or contusion only, but often includes extensive fractures of the cranial vault (top part of the skull) or the basilar skull. It is not uncommon for the fracture lines to be oriented along the direction of impact. Associated intracranial injuries frequently include subarachnoid hemorrhage, brain contusions, diffuse axonal injury and less often, subdural hemorrhage. It should be remembered that a fatal head injury may exist in the absence of skull fractures and, occasionally, any external evidence of injury.

It is valuable for those who investigate RTFs, but whose duties do not include performance of the autopsy, to attend the autopsy. This allows correlation of internal injuries with injuries and markings observed on the body surface and with the circumstances of the incident. With experience, it is often possible to accurately predict the nature of internal injuries based on the findings observed on the body surface.

Artifactual Injuries

Always keep in mind that that the body may be accidentally traumatized during rescue, extrication from the vehicle or transport. For example, the body might be dropped by rescue personnel or struck by the force of a high-pressure fire hose. Sparks that result from the cutting of nearby metal to extricate the victim may cause unusual burns. Such possibilities always must be considered and evaluated as appropriate for the case.

Preparing to Investigate

The *National Guidelines for Death Investigation* include a list of 52 items that are considered basic equipment for potential use. They will not be relisted here; the reader is referred to that publication for further information. In most cases of RTFs, however, a camera, measuring tape, bags for collection of evidence, sheets for use as barriers and for transport of the body, rubber gloves, necessary transport items such as body bags, writing implements (paper and pencil) and communication equipment such as radio or phone are all that will be necessary. One must always be prepared for the worst. For example, investigators may discover that an apparent driver fatality has a bullet hole in the chest — in that case, the investigation abruptly changes from a RTF investigation to a full-blown murder investigation. For such reasons, a scene kit consisting of all items listed in the *National Guidelines* is recommended.

Initial Procedures at the Scene

Upon first arriving at the scene, it is important to properly identify yourself and all others at the scene, and to determine who will be responsible for the various aspects of the investigation. Proper communication and cooperation are essential to a proper investigation.

If the body is in public view, it may be necessary and desirable to construct a barrier of sheeting or other objects that block view of the body from passersby. If the body is in such a position that it poses a safety problem, or is in danger of further impact and mutilation, or is causing a significant traffic flow problem, the body may be moved to a more desirable location.

However, the body should be photographed and the body should be outlined in chalk or with some other suitable marking substance before it is moved.

Of course, it should be ascertained that the victim is indeed dead. Usually, by the time the ME/C or DI is notified, emergency personnel have made that determination. However, it will be necessary to have death officially pronounced by a licensed physician or other person in accordance with provisions of state and local law. In many areas the ME/C or DI may pronounce death, but knowledge of state law is essential.

Primary Investigative Tasks

The ME/C or DI must perform the following tasks at every RTF scene:

- Establish scene safety.
- Confirm that a death has occurred.
- Perform or arrange for pronouncement of death.
- Collect information to establish the identity of the deceased.
- Collect basic demographic data (age, race, sex, address).
- Determine who will notify the next of kin; notify if needed.
- Safeguard the body and associated personal property and potential evidence.
- Arrange for or perform body packaging and transport.
- Determine the reported facts of the incident as determined by the law enforcement agency and compare with personal observations.
- Determine and document (or perform) relevant measurements related to primary and subsequent impact sites and ultimate location of bodies and vehicles. If possible, use the "triangulation" method in which each object's location is measured from the same two fixed points.
- Photograph relevant findings which, at a minimum, include the body in its final position, any damaged areas on the vehicle, and any points of impact of vehicle or body with other objects.
- Document the status of vehicle glass (intact, cracked, shattered, etc).
- Determine if there are any tire marks, especially prior to initial impact site.
- Document identifying features of vehicles (color, make, model, VIN, tag number).
- Determine if there are any indications of possible suicide or homicide and follow up appropriately (see above).
- Determine if there appears to have been adequate impact(s) to cause death or if death appears to be more likely due to natural causes.

- Assist the law enforcement officer in the location and interviewing of witnesses.
- Determine if the victim was on the job at the time of the incident.
- Prepare a written report including necessary diagrams.
- Notify other agencies as required (highway department if a road problem exists, etc.).
- Provide assistance to families (referral for grief counseling, etc.).

If the victim was a driver or other occupant of the vehicle, some additional tasks are needed:

- Attempt to identify and document any points of contact between victim(s) and vehicle interior. This may be helpful not only to clarify how injuries occurred, but also — especially when driver and/or occupants are ejected — to help establish who was the driver and the seating locations of other passengers.
- Determine if vehicle is in gear and, if so, which one.
- Determine if headlight control switch is on.
- Determine if there is any evidence of seat belt use, air bag deployment or damage to safety/restraint devices.
- Determine status of doors (open, closed) prior to manipulation by responders.
- Examine gas and brake pedals for damage or markings; collect brake and gas pedal pads for comparison with possible marks on footwear.

If the victim is a pedestrian or there is evidence of a body having been run over:

- Attempt to determine all impact sites with vehicle(s) and other objects, being sure to take adequate photographs.
- Inspect underside of vehicle for blood, tissue and clothing.
- Document the make and model of the tires, including photographs of relevant tread patterns.

If there is dismemberment or bodily fragmentation:

- Attempt to locate and obtain all fragments, body parts and tissues.

If bodies were ejected from the vehicle:

- Measure, diagram and photograph precise locations of bodies relevant to vehicles and other objects.

- Attempt to identify and document all impact points after ejection.
- Examine vehicle interior to determine if there is any information to establish victim seating location.

As needed :

- Collect clothing (and helmet, if a motorcycle incident).
- Collect hospital admission blood.
- Get copies of medical records, ambulance trip sheets and incident report prepared by the law enforcement agency.
- Obtain further background medical/social/psychiatric information on victim.
- Conduct investigation of other relevant scene locations (home, work site, etc.).

Overall Goals of the Investigation

Although the ME/C or DI may not be primarily responsible for determining all of the facts below, at the conclusion of the investigation, the ME/C and/or DI should have ascertained or have a reasonable understanding of:

- The identity of the deceased
- Demographic data about the deceased
- A reasonable understanding of how the incident occurred and the probable roles of the driver, vehicle, roadway and environment in causing the incident
- The specific nature and extent of injury
- Whether there is any indication of homicide, suicide or natural death
- How specific injuries were sustained (mechanisms)
- The cause and manner of death
- The type of place and address where the incident occurred
- Whether the victim was a driver, occupant (passenger) or pedestrian
- The basic categorization of the crash (car hit fixed object, car-to-car head-on collision, etc.)

The Autopsy and Toxicology Testing

It should be apparent that there are several reasons for performing a complete autopsy when the victim was a driver or pedestrian. This should be done as a matter of routine procedure, if consistent with the law. Whether or not a complete autopsy is performed on other occupants (passengers) depends on the law, available resources and the circumstances of the incident. It is good practice to perform an autopsy on all traffic fatality victims, if possible. In some areas, however, this may not be practical or possible. When such is the case, it is prudent to perform an autopsy if the facts of the incident suggest that there will be criminal prosecution. Autopsy is also desirable if it seems likely that a civil lawsuit may stem from the incident and applicable laws do not preclude an autopsy.

Toxicology testing should be performed on drivers and pedestrians. Which substances to test for depend partially on whether the investigations provide evidence of specific drug use. Ethanol should be routinely tested for. If possible, a drug screen for cocaine, opiates, amphetamines and tranquilizers/sedatives should also be included. It is also prudent to test for carbon monoxide to exclude leakage of exhaust into the passenger compartment. In cases suspicious for suicide, additional tests for psychiatric medications and antidepressants may also be helpful. The extent of toxicology testing on vehicle occupants depends on the case, but routine testing for alcohol and common drugs of abuse (cocaine and opiates) is also reasonable.

References

1. Limpert, R., *Motor Vehicle Accident Reconstruction and Cause Analysis* (4th ed.), Charlottesville, VA: The Michie Company, 1994.

2. U.S. Department of Justice, *National Guidelines for Death Investigation*, Washington, D.C.: National Institute of Justice, December 1997.

3. Spitz, W. and Fisher, R., *Medicolegal Investigation of Death* (2nd ed.), Springfield, IL: Charles C Thomas, 1993.

Figure 1 Major accidents may or may not have associated deaths. Two people died in this head-on collision.

Figure 2 A head-on collision. Expect injuries to the occupant's right side, as if he/she traveled toward the point of impact.

Figure 3 This truck ran into a bridge. Miraculously, the driver walked away from the accident. Unfortunately, his brother, who was in the cab's sleeping compartment, died.

Figure 4 The car came to rest against a pole. The passenger may have "intrusion" injuries from the impacted door.

Figure 5   The driver of this vehicle was caught upside down in his seatbelt and suffocated (postural asphyxiation).

Figure 6   The examiner or investigator should know the position of the decedent in the vehicle.

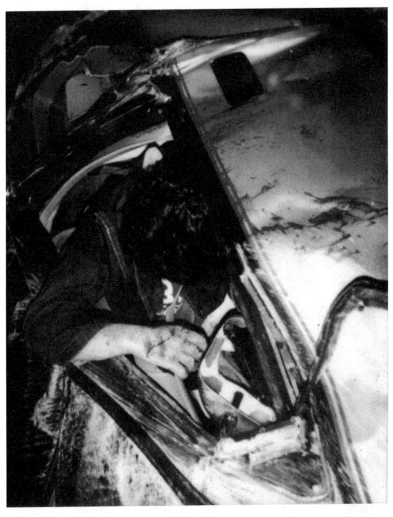

Figure 7 This driver was pinned in the wreckage, and sustained impressive head trauma.

Figure 8   This driver died of a combination of head and chest trauma.

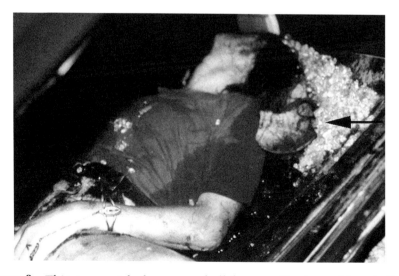

Figure 9   This occupant had an open skull fracture. Portions of her skull are next to her shoulder.

Figure 10   Broken windshield resulting from the impact of the passenger's head.

Figure 11   Emergency personnel are among the first to arrive at the accident scene. They are good sources of information concerning the location of the body/bodies and whether the victims were dead or alive when first viewed.

Figure 12 A van T-boned a smaller vehicle, after which both were damaged by fire. The occupants were also thermally injured.

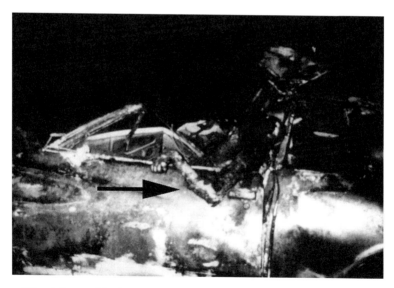

Figure 13 A burned body in the car after the accident and subsequent fire. An autopsy would prove if the person died from the fire or the impact, or a combination of the two.

Figure 14   A close-up of a thermally injured occupant. Most bodies are burned after death. Testing for carbon monoxide in the blood and an examination for soot in the airway will prove if the person was alive or dead at the time of the fire.

Figure 15   Papers and a watch at the scene helped to identify the burned remains
of the driver.

Figure 16 This woman was lying outside the car. Was she in this position when first discovered? The investigator must speak with the first people to arrive at the scene.

Figure 17 One of the occupants of the accident vehicle was thrown out of the car. It is important to decide if he was driving.

Figure 18   Careful examination of the vehicle may reveal areas on or in the car where the occupant made contact. There is brain material in this door frame.

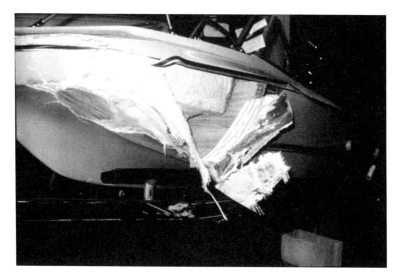

Figure 19   The damage to this boat occurred after it became unhitched while being towed. It traveled across the median and struck a Volkswagen head-on, killing the driver of the car.

Figure 20 The driver of this vehicle was intoxicated, missed a turn, and drove into the pond. He drowned. There were no bodily injuries.

Figure 21 This truck traveled under a parked tractor trailer, decapitating the driver. The point of impact of the driver's head on the truck was apparent.

Figure 22 The grass and weeds stuck in this grill indicate of how the truck rolled after the accident.

Figure 23 Skid marks are helpful when determining whether or not a death was an accident or suicide.

Figure 24 Faint tire marks on the sidewalk. This finding helped in reconstructing a hit-and-run homicide.

Figure 25 Scrape marks of the vehicle on the median concrete divider.

Figure 26   Impact site on the concrete from the driver's head.

Figure 27   Motorcyclists are sometimes told to aim for an animal in the road. If they do, chances are they will miss the animal. Unfortunately, that did not work this time. The motorcyclist died after hitting the deer at an estimated speed of 70 mph. He died of head trauma; he was wearing a helmet.

Figure 28   This vehicle traveled straight into a tree. This was a suicide. The driver also had incised wounds on one of his wrists.

Figure 29   The driver of this car drove her vehicle into a rock wall. See next photo.

Figure 30 The stuck speedometer indicates how fast the car was traveling when it hit the wall. See next photo.

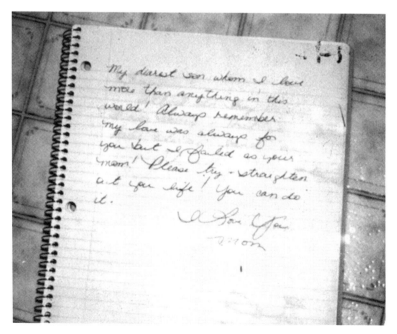

Figure 31 A suicide note was discovered in the trunk.

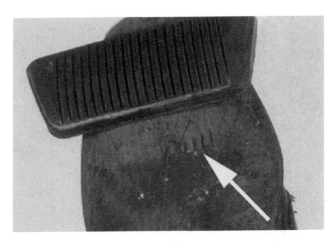

Figure 32   Leather sole shoes may have impressions from the brake or accelerator pedals. This may give a clue as to how the driver was reacting at the time of the accident.

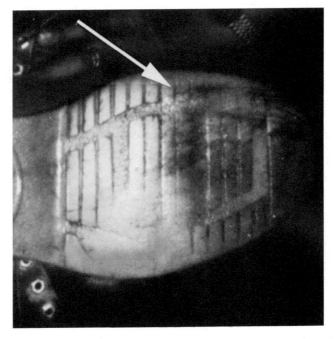

Figure 33   Pedal marks on the sole. These are not distinct enough to distinguish between the brake and accelerator pedals.

Figure 34   The initial site of a high-speed impact. The distance from the impact site to the body's location gives an indication of the vehicle's speed at the moment of impact. See next photo.

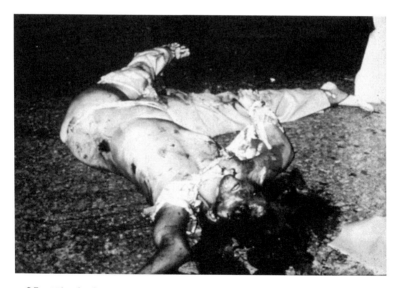

Figure 35   The body came to rest yards away from the impact site.

Figure 36 Pedestrians may be struck multiple times, especially on highways. Initial impact sites may be difficult to evaluate.

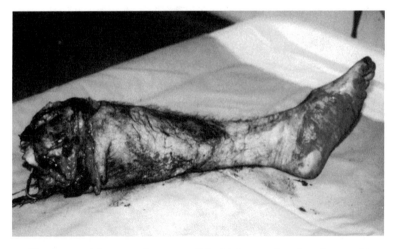

Figure 37 Extremities may be torn off in high-speed pedestrian accidents.

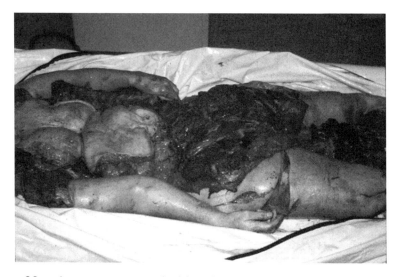

Figure 38   This person was crushed from being run over. Such extensive injuries make it difficult to identify impact sites.

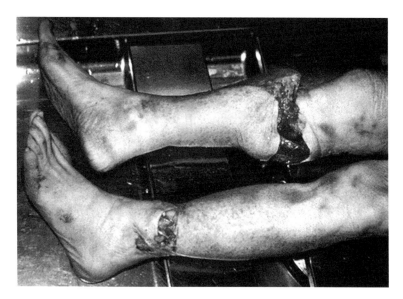

Figure 39   The heights of fractures must be measured. The fracture heights may be matched to bumper heights. The distances may indicate whether or not the vehicle was braking at the time of impact. See next photo.

Figure 40   This is the vehicle that struck the man in the previous photo. The bumper height can be matched to the height of the fractures.

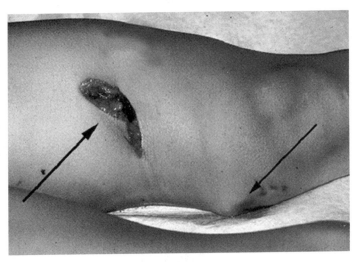

Figure 41   Fractured bones may not match the external sites of impact. The impact site in the thigh area is quite far from the end of the fracture. The impact site is more important than the location of the end of the fracture.

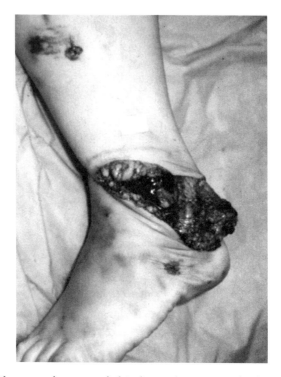

Figure 42   The open fracture of this lower leg occurred when the pedestrian was struck; at the time, this leg was in contact with the ground.

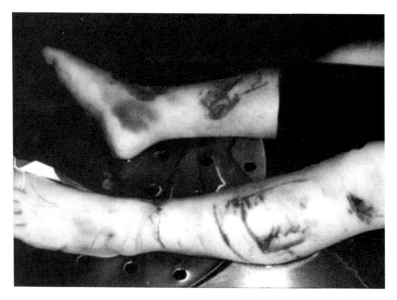

Figure 43   Multiple points of impact from being struck during a hit-and-run. There are pattern injuries that can be matched to the vehicle.

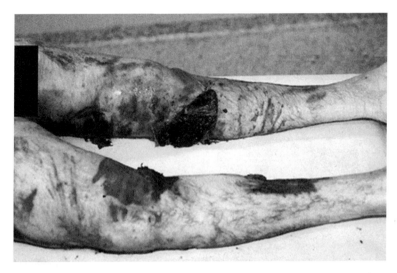

Figure 44   Pedestrian. Extensive injuries of the legs and pelvis from the initial impact.

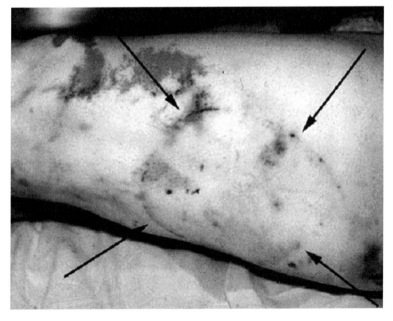

Figure 45   Patterns from the vehicle may be present. The arrows outline a headlight on this man's leg.

Figure 46 Damaged areas on a vehicle may need to be examined because the area may be matched to injuries on the body.

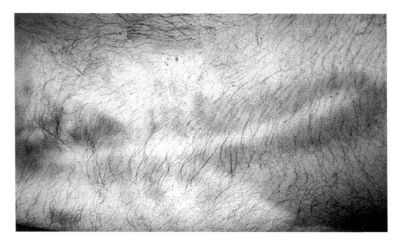

Figure 47 This pedestrian was struck by a truck. Paint chips on the clothing and this mark with the pale center on his leg helped to identify the particular type of truck.

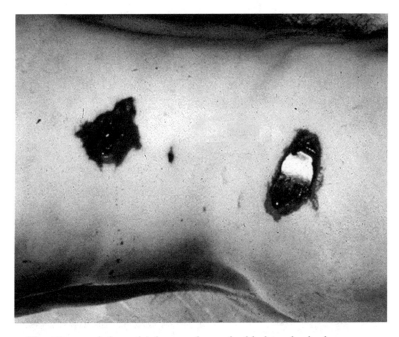

Figure 48   Pieces of the vehicle may be embedded in the body.

Figure 49   Pedestrian. Clothing may be disoriented and pulled off. Some people may be "knocked out" of their shoes.

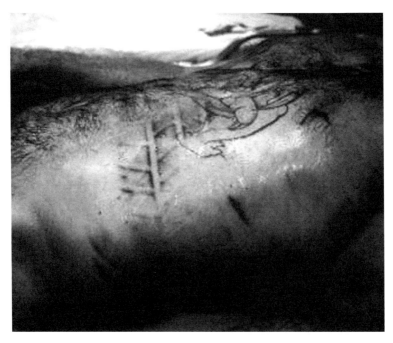

Figure 50 Sharply defined tire markings on the chest and abdomen. These marks can be matched to the tire that caused the injury.

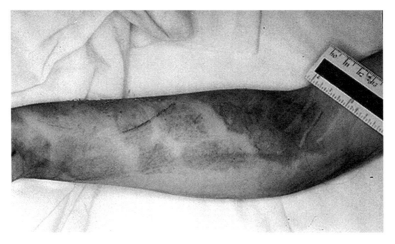

Figure 51   Tire mark on the right arm.

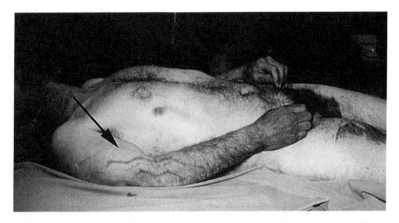

Figure 52   Another tire pattern on an arm.

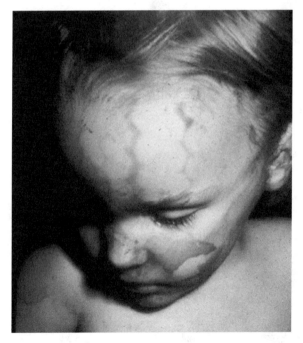

Figure 53   The tread pattern on the child's head may be matched to the vehicle that struck him.

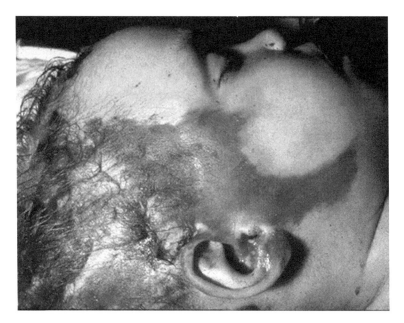

Figure 54 These marks were caused by a tire stretching the skin.

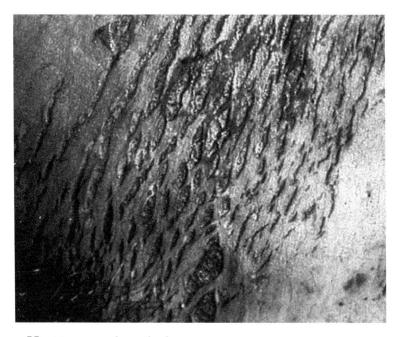

Figure 55 More stretch marks from a tire.

Figure 56 Pedestrian. Pattern paint mark from the vehicle.

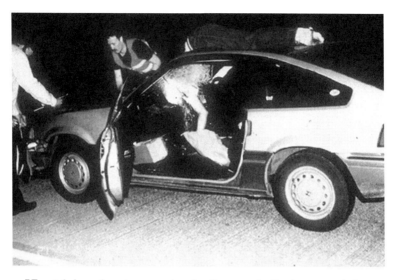

Figure 57 Adult pedestrians tend to be "run under" when struck by automobiles. This man was struck and lifted into the air, and came to rest on the car's top and windshield. See next photo.

Figure 58 A closer view of the body's final resting position.

Figure 59   Pedestrians may receive injuries from striking the vehicle after being thrown into the air. There may also be secondary impact sites on the vehicles.

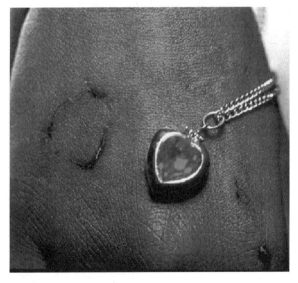

Figure 60   The girl wearing this bracelet was struck with such force that the pendant abraded the skin. See next photo.

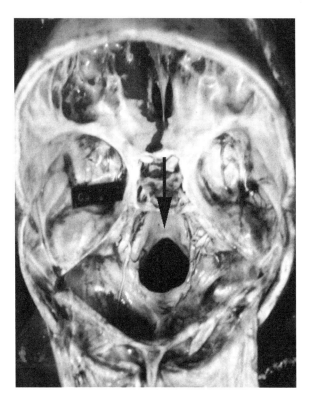

Figure 61 The force of the impact was so great that the vertebral column was completely torn away from the base of the skull. No spinal cord is visible in the foramen where it is normally located (arrow).

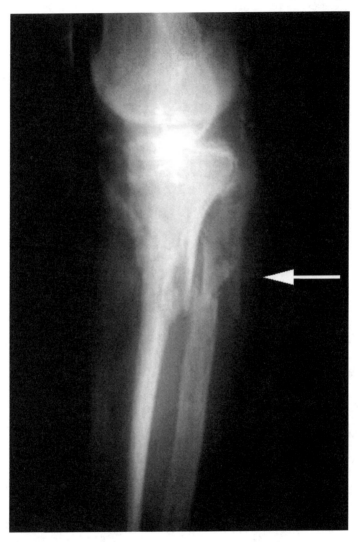

Figure 62   Pedestrian. X-ray of fractured leg at the impact site.

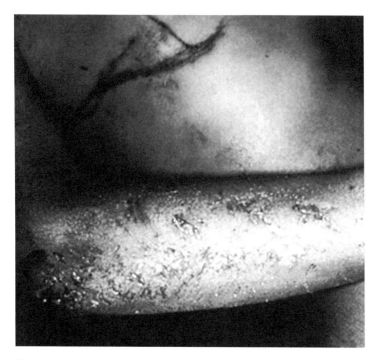

Figure 63   Impact lacerations and abrasions from the roadway.

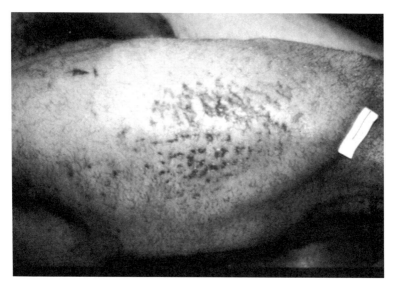

Figure 64   Pebble abrasions from the roadway.

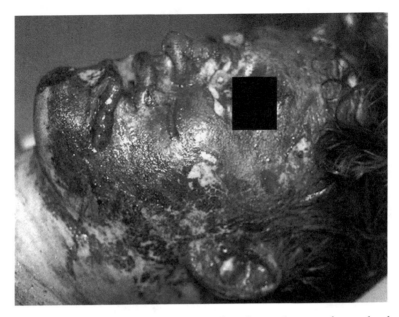

Figure 65 Road rash of the face. The rougher the roadway surfaces, the deeper and more impressive the injuries.

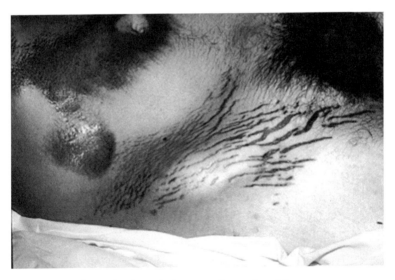

Figure 66 Stretch marks from being struck on the side.

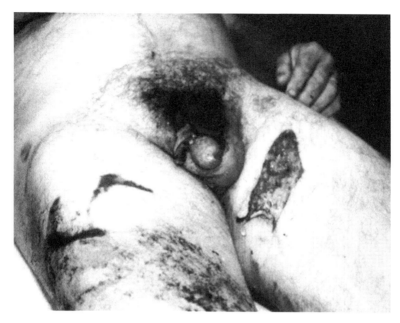

Figure 67 Lacerations of the scrotum with evisceration of the testicle. There was no direct impact to the scrotum. The pressure from the force of the impact caused the skin rupture.

Figure 68 This scalp with ear was discovered on the truck involved in a hit-and-run.

Figure 69 This boy was decapitated after a hit-and-run. The distance of the head from the body helped determine the speed of the car.

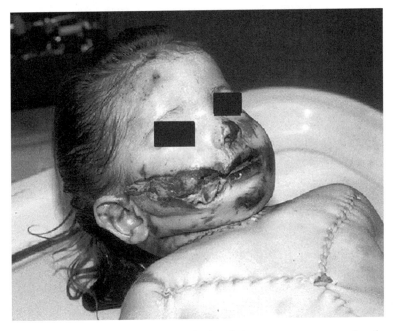

Figure 70 The boy's head was reattached and there was an open casket funeral.

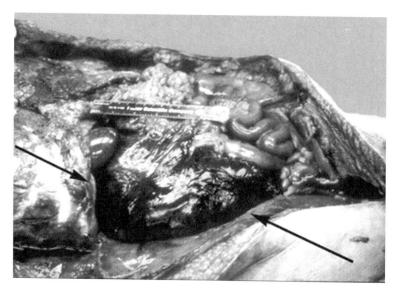

Figure 71 Retroperitoneal hemorrhage. This state trooper was struck by a drunk driver's car while issuing a ticket to another drunk driver.

Figure 72 Pieces of paint and other material found on clothing are important to collect. They may be matched to missing areas on a vehicle, as in this case.

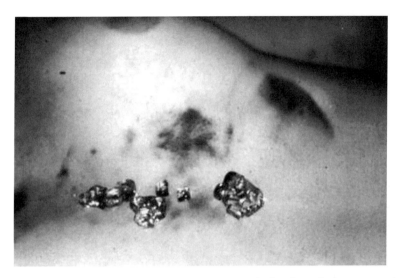

Figure 73   Glass fragments caused these irregularly shaped abrasions of the chest.

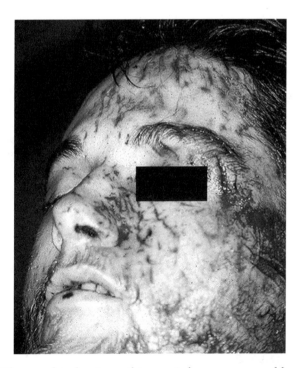

Figure 74   The angulated cuts on this man's face were caused by contact with the side window. The tempered glass making up the side window fractured in cubes. These injuries are called "dicing abrasions," or "glass dicing."

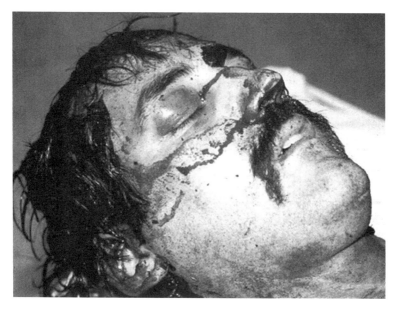

Figure 75   The black eyes (spectacle hemorrhages) were caused by blood seeping down into the face from fractures of the skull above the eyes.

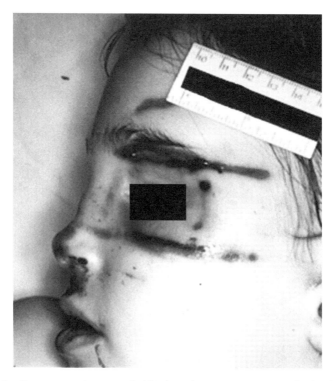

Figure 76   Pattern marks on a child's face from an impact with the dashboard.

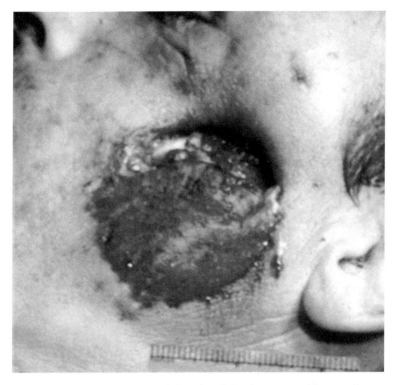

Figure 77   Pattern mark on the left side of the face caused by a pole.

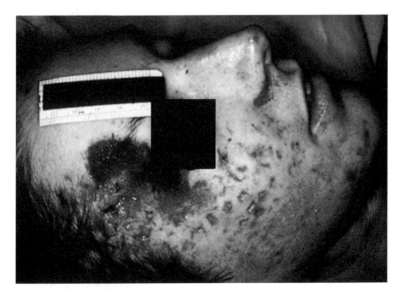

Figure 78   Dicing abrasions on the face of a passenger.

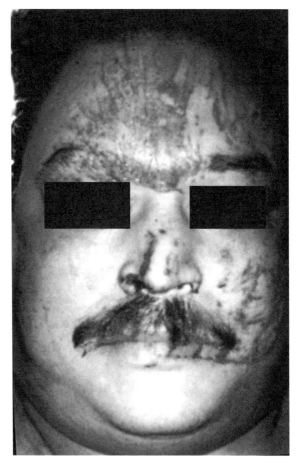

Figure 79   This man's forehead is abraded and torn from an impact with the windshield.

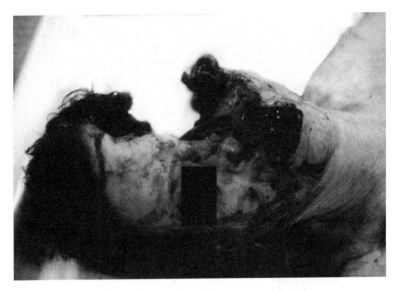

Figure 80 Woman struck by a pole while a passenger in a car.

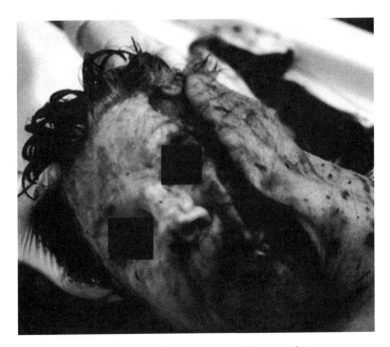

Figure 81 Woman hit by the edge of a sign while seated in a car.

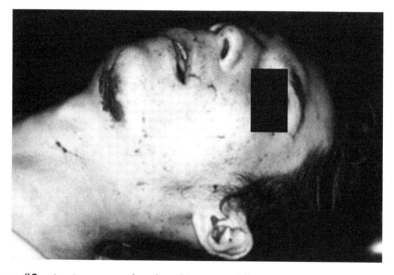

Figure 82   An impact under the chin caused hyperextension injuries to the spinal cord and brain.

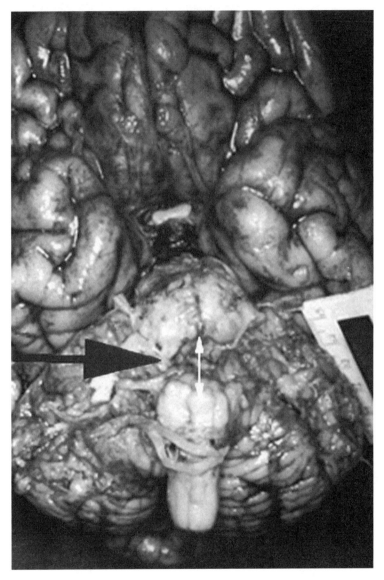

Figure 83 Transection of the brainstem between the medulla and pons (arrow). This type of injury occurs in a violent hyperextension of the head.

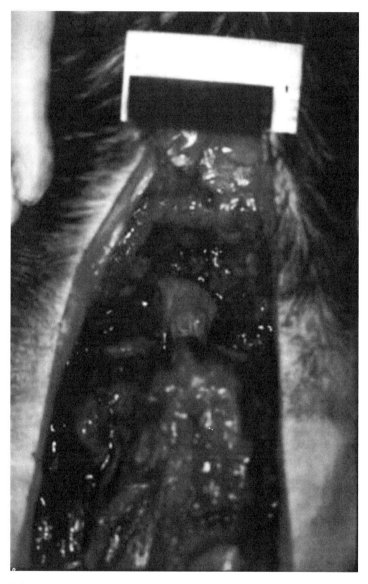

Figure 84   Extensive soft tissue hemorrhage in the back of the neck from a severe whiplash or hyperextension injury.

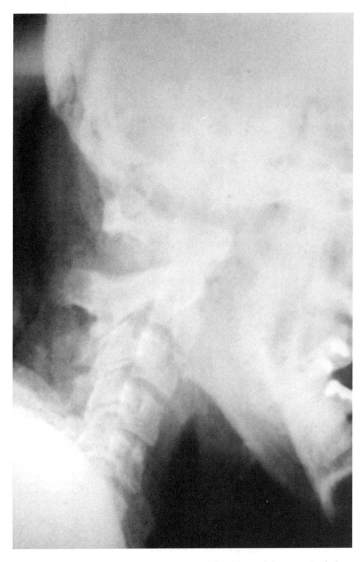

Figure 85 X-ray of the neck revealing a subluxation (slippage) of the vertebral column. This type of injury causes sudden death by impingement of the spinal cord. Actual fractures of the cervical vertebral column are not as common as thought.

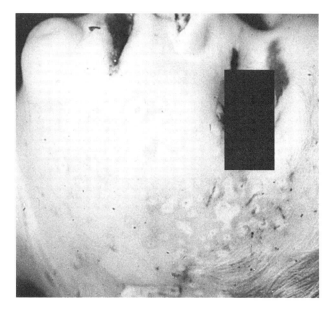

Figure 86   Child with burn marks on the face.

Figure 87   The driver died after ejection when his head hit the tree.

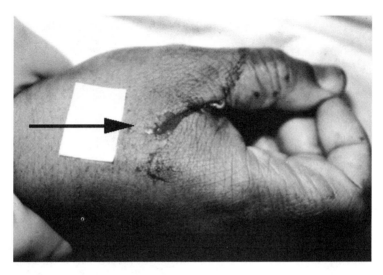

Figure 88 Laceration in the web of the hand. This indicated the driver was holding the steering wheel during impact.

Figure 89 Air bags may prevent external injuries. This woman died from a ruptured aorta after the accident. She had no external injuries.

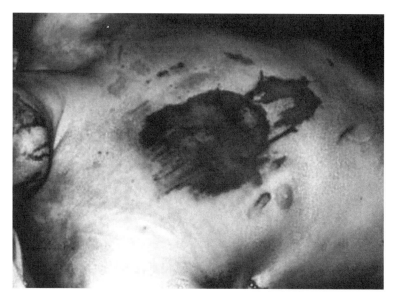

Figure 90   This is the type of external injury typically resulted from impacting the steering column in head-on collisions, and was common prior to the use of seat belts and air bags.

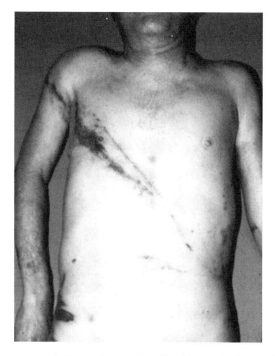

Figure 91   Pattern seatbelt marks on the shoulder and chest of a passenger.

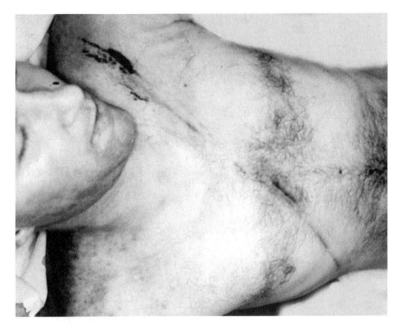

Figure 92   Seatbelt marks on a driver.

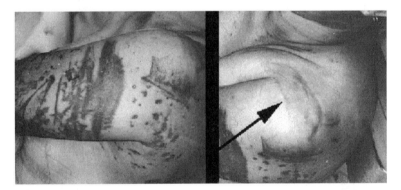

Figure 93   These photos of a vehicle occupant reveal injuries to the shoulder and upper arm. The arrow points to the mark made by a seat belt, which proves the decedent was the driver.

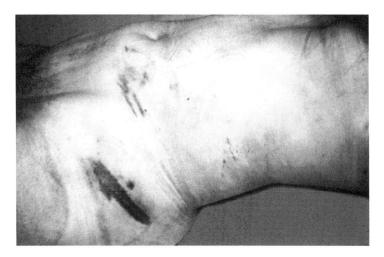

Figure 94   Abrasions from a seat (lap) belt.

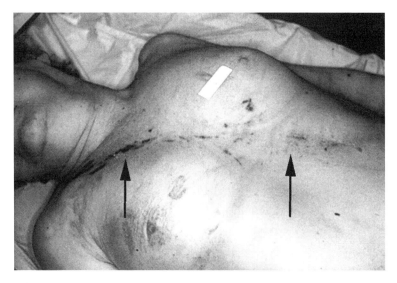

Figure 95   Slight abrasions of the chest from the seatbelt.

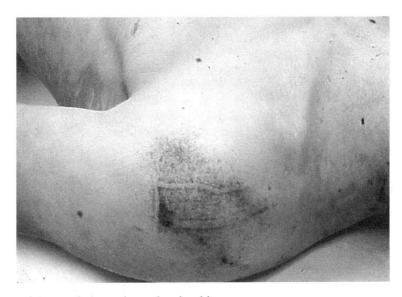

Figure 96   Seatbelt mark on the shoulder.

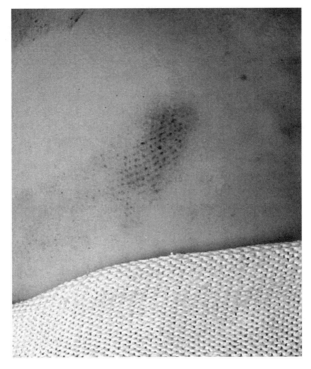

Figure 97   The pattern of the clothing can be seen on the skin.

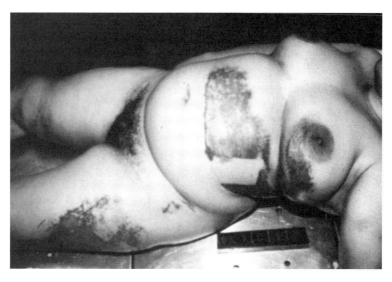

Figure 98   The abraded areas were caused by the decedent's clothing.

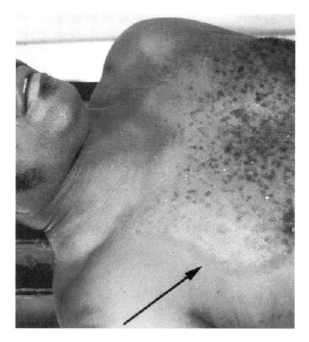

Figure 99   The only mark on this man's body was this contusion from a truck's cab. He was trapped after he attempted to jump clear of the truck as it began to roll over. He died of asphyxiation.

Figure 100 The driver was ejected and pinned after the truck overturned. There were numerous petechiae and prominent congestion of the face from compression.

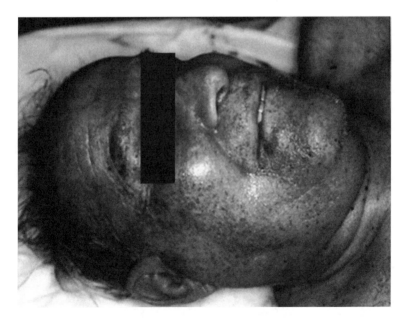

Figure 101 Congestion of the face from compression asphyxia.

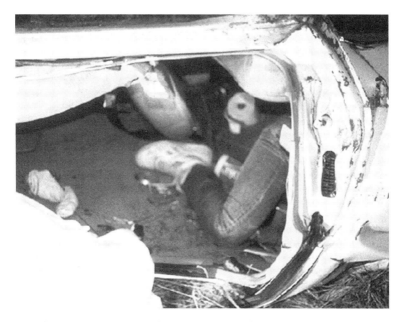

Figure 102 In this accident, the car overturned and one of the passengers was discovered dead, lying in this position. See next photo.

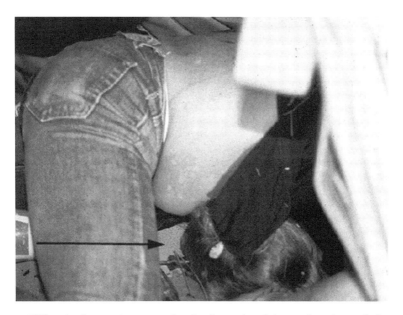

Figure 103 A closer view reveals the boy's head (arrow) to be tightly compressed against his chest. He died from positional asphyxiation.

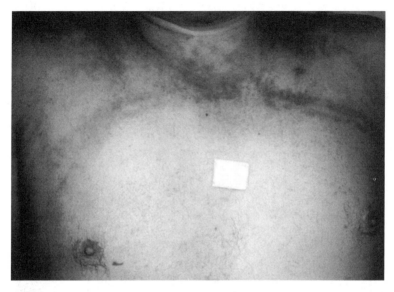

Figure 104   Pressure marks across the uper chest from compression.

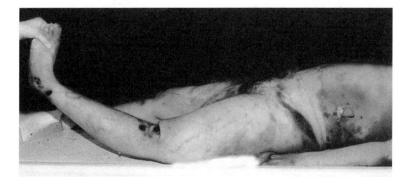

Figure 105   This driver had a fracture of the leg and many other nonspecific injuries.

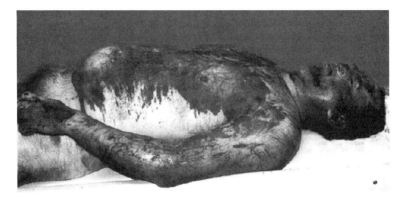

Figure 106   This is an example of "road rash" after the man was ejected from the vehicle and slid across the road.

Figure 107   Impaled during ejection.

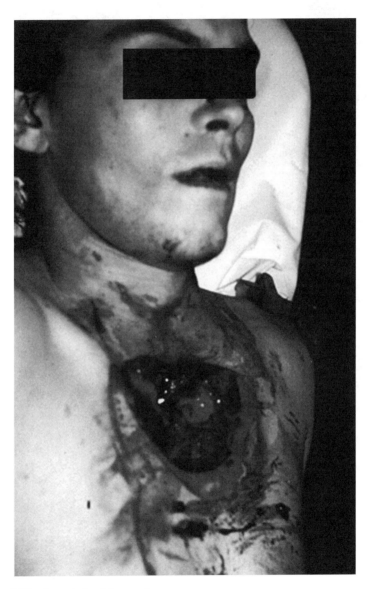

Figure 108 Impaled with a pole.

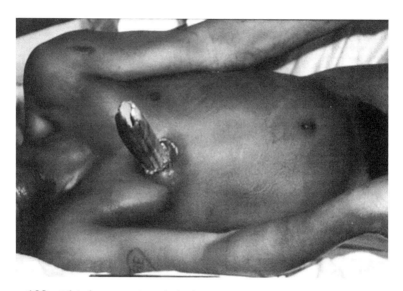

Figure 109   This boy was impaled after ejection.

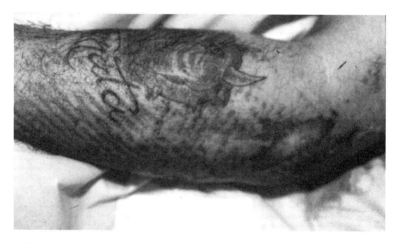

Figure 110   Linear abrasions from the roadway.

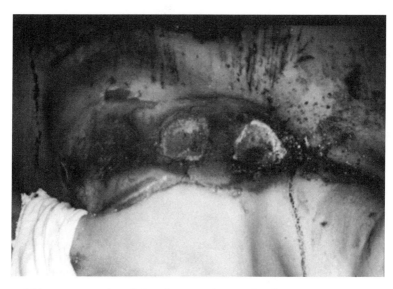

Figure 111   Burn marks of the chest as the result of an ejection and rollover.

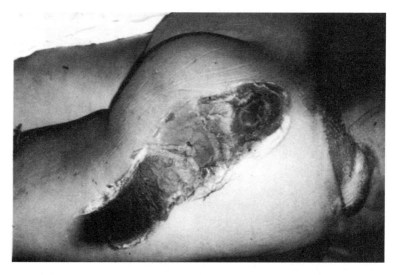

Figure 112   Burns on the hip and buttocks from a muffler, which occurred during a rollover.

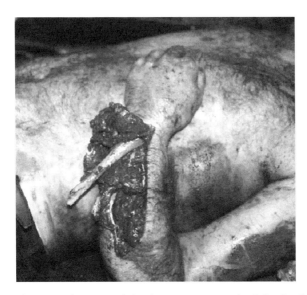

Figure 113   This open fracture of the forearm occurred while the driver grabbed the steering wheel.

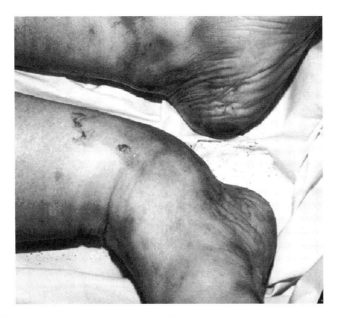

Figure 114   Closed fractures of the ankles.

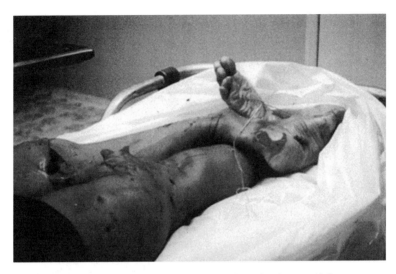

Figure 115   Lower leg and ankle fractures after the legs and feet were caught under the seat during a head-on collision.

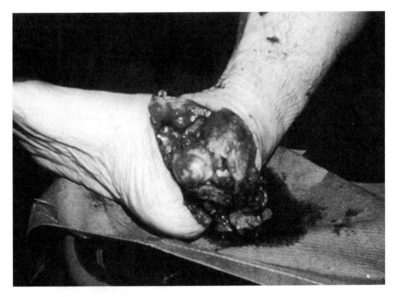

Figure 116   Open fracture of the ankle occurred after the foot was caught under the seat.

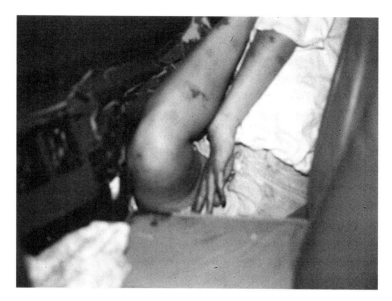

Figure 117   Fracture of the femur at the scene. This scene photo leaves little doubt as to the cause of the fracture.

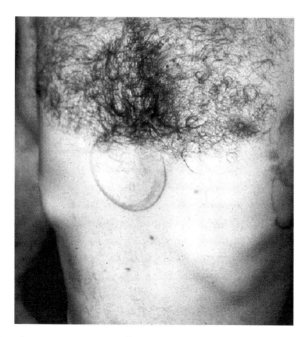

Figure 118   This is not an injury from the steering wheel. It is an abrasion that resulted from shocking the decedent during CPR. Note similar marks on the left side of the chest.

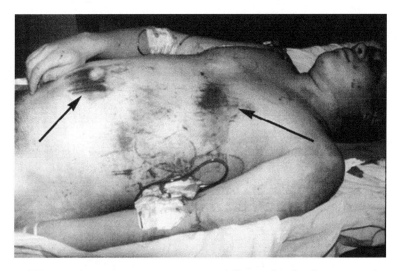

Figure 119 Occupants may sustain many different kinds of injuries. This man had some pattern marks on the abdomen that were matched to part of the seat in the car.

Figure 120 Extensive lacerations of the liver from an impact with the abdomen and lower chest.

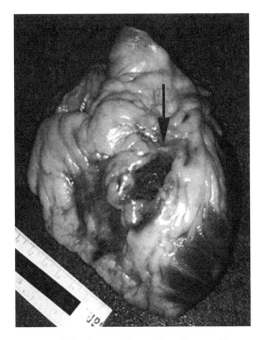

Figure 121   Laceration of the heart after a head-on collision.

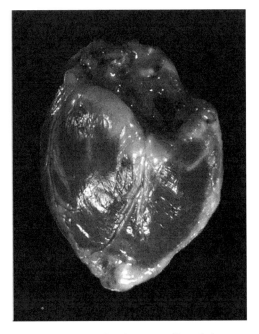

Figure 122   This heart was completely torn off and discovered floating in the left chest cavity after a head-on collision.

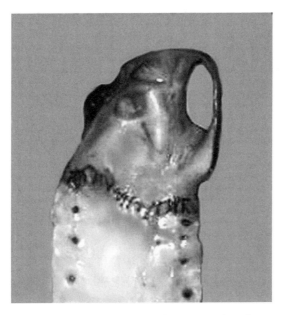

Figure 123   This sutured laceration in the aorta of a driver is in the area commonly torn during a frontal or side impact.

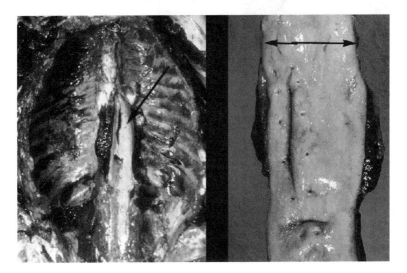

Figure 124   This is an unusual tear in the aorta. The tear is usually horizontal and not vertical.

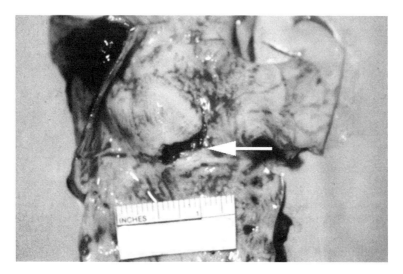

Figure 125   Laceration of the aorta after a head-on collision.

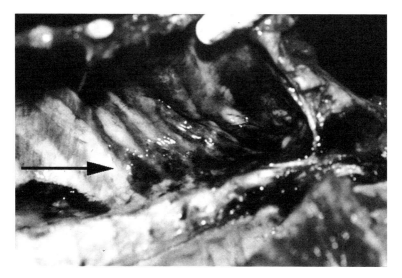

Figure 126   There may be multiple rib fractures and soft tissue bleeding in any impact to the chest.

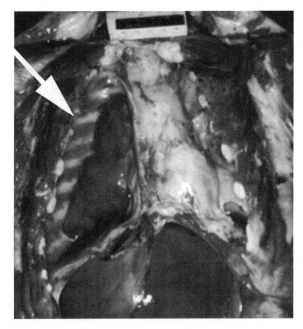

Figure 127   A child with a collapsed right lung. Note how far the lung has collapsed away from the chest wall. This is an indication there was a build-up of air in the chest cavity.

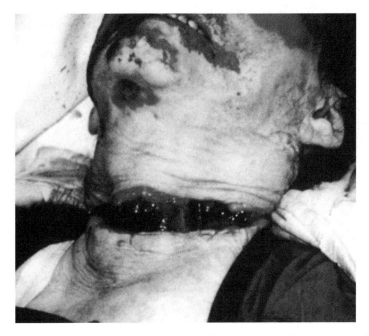

Figure 128   A cutting injury of the neck that occurred during an accident. It looks as if a knife caused the injury.

Figure 129   Hemorrhage in the soft tissue behind the ear (Battle's sign) is an indication of a skull fracture.

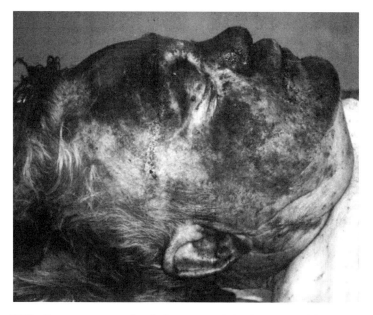

Figure 130   Extensive superficial abrasions of the face caused by being thrown around the inside of a tractor. See next photo.

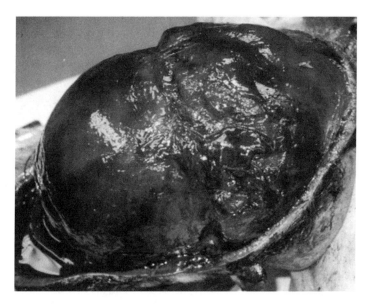

Figure 131 Extensive subscalpular hemorrhage from the multiple impacts. There was no trauma to the brain.

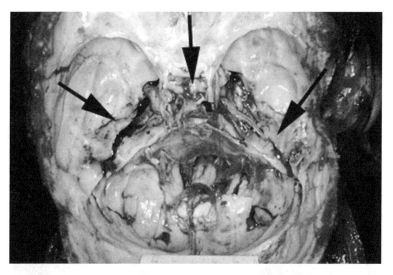

Figure 132 Fractures of the skull in the areas indicated by arrows will cause bleeding in the ear canals. There may be an associated bluish discoloration of the skin behind the ears (Battle's sign).

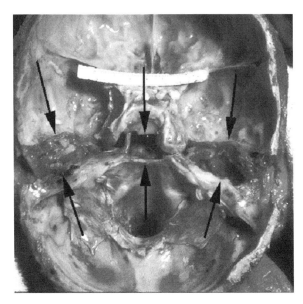

Figure 133   A hinged fracture of the skull. External examination would indicate blood in the decedent's ear canals.

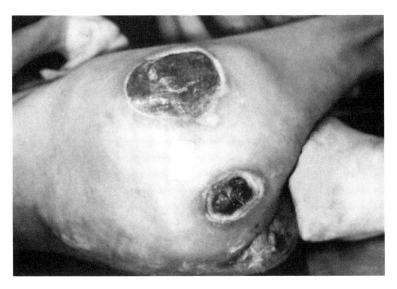

Figure 134   Not all victims die right away. This person has multiple pressure sores (*decubitus ulcers*) and died from infection long after the accident. The death is still considered a complication of the accident.

Figure 135 This accident did not appear serious; however, the driver was dead. See next photo.

Figure 136 There was no damage to the vehicle or apparent injury to the driver. Autopsy revealed the driver died of a heart attack. When an accident is minor and the driver is dead, the investigator must first consider a natural cause.

Figure 137   This was the scene of a head-on collision. See next photo.

Figure 138   The driver's wife, seated on the passenger side, had a broken arm only. See next photo.

Figure 139 The driver was caught in the cab. The extrication took over an hour and the man survived for only a short time in the emergency room. Knowledge of the scene is important for understanding the cause of death.

Figure 140 A car left the right side of the roadway at this curve. The highway patrol estimated the car's speed at 40 to 45 mph when it left the road. See next photo.

Figure 141 The car came to rest in the adjacent field and the driver was dead in the front seat. The arrow points to a ruler, which measures the size of the open window. The driver's hat was discovered next to a fence at the point of initial impact. See next photo.

Figure 142 The driver was discovered with his head below the passenger's seat. This was the only area of blood in the car. See next photo.

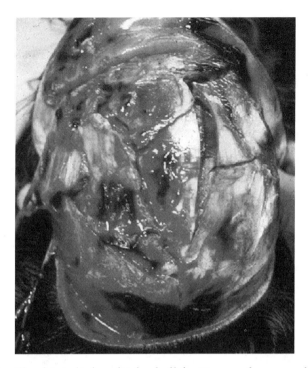

Figure 143 The driver had multiple skull fractures and an open laceration of the scalp from a frontal impact; however, there were no points of impact seen inside the car. Such cases remain a mystery.

Figure 144 A boy was riding his bicycle home after work one night. The back wheel of the bicycle revealed he was struck from behind. The body was not at the scene of initial impact. See next photo.

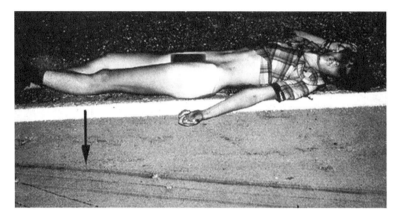

Figure 145   The body was discovered approximately 3 miles from the site of the accident. The line of blood next to the body could be followed for 2.5 miles. See next photo.

Figure 146   There were considerable injuries to his side from being dragged. See next photo.

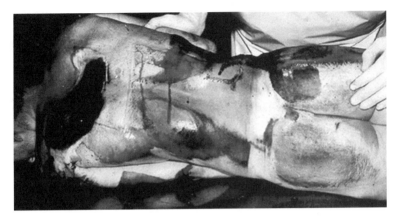

Figure 147 There were black rubbing marks from the tires of the truck. The only significant injuries to the body were those from being dragged. See next photo.

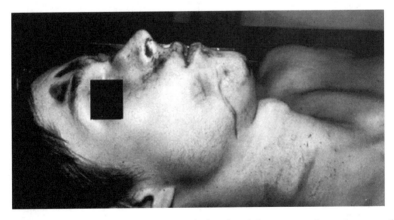

Figure 148 There were abrasions of the face; however, there was no head trauma. See next photo.

Figure 149   The truck was discovered in a trailer park. The owner was inside. See next photo.

Figure 150   The truck showed signs that the bike was struck by the front of the truck. See next photo.

Figure 151 The driver's shoes were in the sink. He had attempted to wash them. Blood on the shoes matched that of the decedent. The driver had no license and had been convicted three times for drunk driving. He was sent to jail for 25 years.

Figure 152 Most motorcyclists die from head trauma even if they are wearing helmets.

Figure 153 The body tends to be thrown free of the motorcycle and impact against the ground.

Figure 154 Some helmets, such as this one, are more protective because they cover the entire head. However, at high rates of speed, helmets do not guard against serious injury.

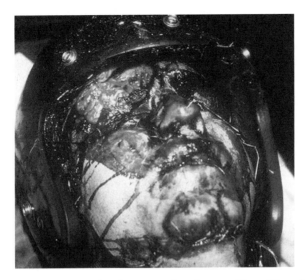

Figure 155   This motorcyclist hit a tree head-on at 50 to 55 mph.

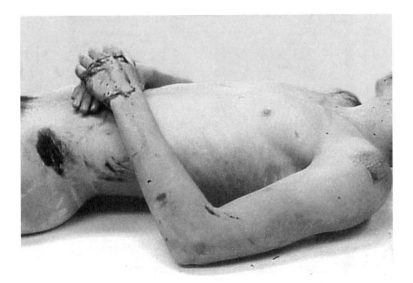

Figure 156   This 15-year-old was the passenger in a car that went out of control, flipped and hit a tree. He was belted in. There were few external signs of trauma. Notice the lap belt mark on his hip. See next photo.

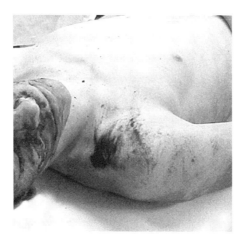

Figure 157   He also had a belt mark on his right shoulder. See next photo.

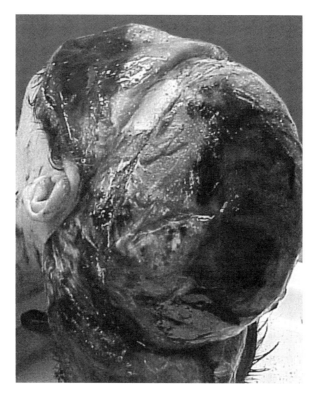

Figure 158   There was marked hemorrhage under the scalp and over the skull; however, there were no skull fractures or brain damage. There were no injuries inside the chest or abdomen. The back of his neck was examined. See next photo.

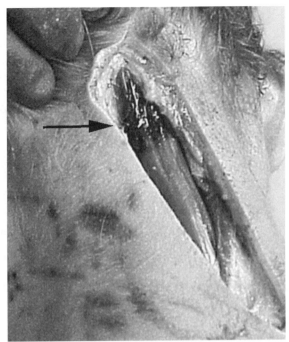

Figure 159   There was blood in the soft tissue high in the neck under the skin.

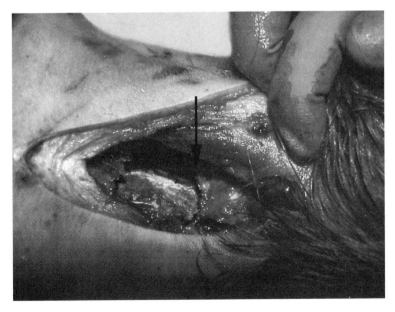

Figure 160   A deeper cut reveals a tearing of the ligaments and a marked displacement of the vertebral column. Subsequent examination revealed the spinal cord had been severed. Occasionally, injuries to the neck may only be detected by examining the back of the neck.

Figure 161 This car skidded off the highway, traveled down an embankment and ended up in the stream. See next photo.

Figure 162 The driver was not in the burned car. See next photo.

Figure 163   The driver was discovered on the hill. Both he and the surrounding area had been burned. Autopsy revealed no soot in the airway and no carbon monoxide in his blood. There were no injuries to the body except for the thermal damage. He died from being compressed as the car rolled over him.